Metamorphosis Love:

PLEASANT DREAMS & WISHES

Vol. 2

Vanessa F. McCoy

Copyright ©2015 Vanessa F. McCoy

All rights reserved. No part of this publication may be reproduced, stored in a retrieval system or transmitted in any form or by any means- electronic, mechanical, photocopy, recording or any other-except for brief quotations in printed reviews, without prior permission of the author.

Edited by Jai JadaJsonos

Printed in the United States of America

Second Printing, 2019

CreateSpace

4900 LaCross Road

North Charleston, SC 29406

www.createspace.com

ISBN: 978-1-7337941-2-1
ISBN – 13: 978-1-7337941-2-1

Metamorphosis – transformed person or thing – somebody or something that has gone through a complete or marked change.

Preface

I wrote poems to my second true love when we were dating. This kind of love was on a new level. A level I had never experienced before even when intimacy wasn't involved. I wrote poems periodically and they eventually became another chapter of my life. I stopped writing over a period of time, but God stirred my spirit in 2014 to publish these poems and get back to doing what I love to do....writing.

Metamorphosis Love is a collection of poems about my true love transitioning from my relationship with men to my relationship with God.

TABLE OF CONTENTS

My New Friend 3
Trust? 5
The Lost Joy 7
Happy 24th Birthday 8
Just a Dream..Or is it Real 10
Turning The Hands Of Time 12
What Would You Do For Love 14
Truth & Happiness 16
Sweet Senses 19
My Midnight Wish 22
Soul Mate 24
Listening To The Beats 26
How Do You… 27
You Remind Me… 29
Am I Suppose To? 30
Do I, Should I 32
Feelings 33
Your Eyes 34
When You 35
A Good Day 36
Remember 37
Notes 40

My New Friend

I have a friend that's dear to me

bringing joy and happiness

This is something he can see

and it makes me feel like I'm blessed

He brightens up my day

just by letting me be me

And takes the sorrow away

so I can feel like I'm free

We can talk about serious issues

and have the surprise look of really

Yet we may need some tissue

from giggling ourselves silly

Vanessa F. McCoy

We can daydream about things

and be on the same wavelength

Because of the joy it brings

that's where I get my happy strength

He has a place in my heart

with his sunshine, oh I can't pretend

This is an excellent start

for my new friend.

Trust?

Where does the trust begin

if you have a closed door?

When does the honesty kick in

if you refuse to accept more?

When does the friend come around

so I can express my feelings to thee?

When does the wall come down

so you can really see?

It wasn't easy for me to do

but I took a daring chance

To spend a wonderful day with you

instead of thinking about it through a glance

Vanessa F. McCoy

I took a chance to trust you

and I don't regret it

It steered my feelings away from blue

and that's a day I won't forget

I wouldn't know more about you

if I didn't give you the time of the day

To be a caring friend that's true

since you talk to me every day.

The Lost Joy

As I sit here in the night

I think of the joy I had

it was a temporary sight

perhaps that's why I'm sad

yet, nobody will ever know

why my face has that look

which will continue to grow

until my feeling is shook

so far away from me

to make me happy

like I used to be

when I was once free.

Vanessa F. McCoy

HAPPY 24TH BIRTHDAY

Life is a precious gift

as a child enters the world

And into a family it will lift

the happy spirits as it unfurls.

Today is not a normal day

for you to do regular things

It's too wonderful for you to lay

because this is what it brings.

A light to shine on you

as you and your family celebrate this day

Because it won't be blue

as you do whatever you may.

A sparkle in your eye

showing the happiness and joy

As you hold back not to cry

because it's your day to enjoy.

There's a gift greater than love

in which you can't ask for more

It's given to you from the one up above

that makes you twenty-four.

On this enlightening day

I wish you peace today

And many more to come as I say

Happy 24th Birthday.

Vanessa F. McCoy

Just a Dream..Or is it Real

As I toss and turn in my bed
I continue to dream my dream
About something in my head
that's real or so it seem

I'm greeted by a young guy
who's amused by my looks
And I can't help but wonder why
since I look like I'm into books

Days past by as we talk to each other
sharing joy and laughter over the phone
As if we're sister and brother
but that was then because now it's gone

Can it be just a dream

or can it be real

Because it seem

like something I can feel

We had so much fun

being nothing more than friends

Until we met one on one

and the fun had to end

Our friendship was turning

into something more hilarious

That would have given us a yearning

to be a little more serious

Should it be a dream

regardless of how I feel

Even though it seem

like it should be real

Vanessa F. McCoy

Turning The Hands Of Time

If I could turn back the hands of time

I would do it for you

I would...

make you happy every second

by fulfilling the wishes you beckon

make your eyes glow

as I love you very slow

fulfill your deepest desire

that's hotter than fire

bring joy into your life

by being your one and only wife

you would laugh, cry, or maybe

just smile, for having a baby

If I could freeze time in a heart beat

   I would hold you very tight

As both of our eyes meet

   love would continue through the night

Vanessa F. McCoy

What Would You Do For Love

If I said I love you

    would you believe me

Would it make you glow inside

    as you stare me down cautiously

Would your true feelings be put aside

    as you pat my hand in an honest way

Would your deepest desire burn bright

    as you try to keep a steady voice

Would you feel unease in the light

    as you shift slowly in your chair

What would you honestly do

    as you stare at me without a clue

If I said that I love you

    since our relationship grew

Into something deeper and new

    that we both know is very true...

Vanessa F. McCoy

Truth & Happiness

Do you know what you do

   to make me act so true

Can you see

   you make me happy

Do you know

   you make me glow

Can you feel

   my happiness is real

Just by being you

   I can enjoy being me

As our feelings continue to be true

   we shall always be happy

*Y*et we can be sad

   when things make us mad

*W*e can feel pain

   and even want to cry

*B*ut what will we gain

   if we don't even try

*T*o bring out the best in this

   and make us happy always

*A*s we stand strong to dismiss

   the sad and painful days

*A*s we lay the truth out on the table

   our true feelings become once again stable

*A*s we shout for joy and smile with glee

   we can continue to be so happy

Vanessa F. McCoy

I can choose to be glad

   and act like I'm free

Or I can choose to be sad

   and let things get the best of me

*H*appiness is my choice

   when I hear your voice

Because you're like a bright shining sun

   producing nothing but laughter, joy, and fun

Sweet Senses

As I lay here in my bed

things swarm around in my head

These thoughts are very special to me

like my friend I think of so heavenly

As I stare at the light that's dim

I lie on my back and think about him

I feel the power in his dark brown eyes

as he looks straight through me,

making me feel mesmerized

His masculine hands release the unbearable stress

and makes me feel like I've been blessed

His taste is delightful

but the flowing juices make it insightful

His smell is so great and incredible

that I see fireworks by the load

if only it was edible

I could feel myself explode

His skin is as soft as a baby's face

it gives a warm sense of grace

that cannot be replaced

His serene voice gently rocks me to sleep

as he sings songs I would love to keep

Metamorphosis Love: Pleasant Dreams & Wishes Vol. 2

He makes my thoughts feel so sweet

and once again.. my senses are complete.

Vanessa F. McCoy

My Midnight Wish

I wish to lay under you and inhale your delightful aroma, as it sends me in a trance of sitting by the ocean on a warm, breezy day, admiring the beauty surrounding me.

The sun embraces me with a warm touch and the wind whispers sweet nothings in my ear. While faint whispers are heard coming from the tree above me. The golden waves applaud as they watch with excitement.

Suddenly, the sun slides under a blanket to sleep for the night and the motionless waves are no longer golden. I feel like everything has deserted me, except for the wind swaying gently in my ears. The moon stands quietly behind me as the grass leans over and caresses my legs.

The silver waves waltz slowly towards me and the tree bends down to tap me on the shoulder. It whispers so that only I can hear it and I turn around with wonder and excitement. The moon is no longer there and I feel lonely again as I drop my head. The tree reaches out and lifts my head to the air above me. I see a strange, yet familiar shadow that wants to join me in the middle of the night. The moon stands proudly above everything as the shadow grows bigger and becomes more visible. He leans forward and smiles as he notices the twinkle in my eyes. He reaches out for my hand and says, "Your Midnight Wish, Shall Be Fulfilled".

Vanessa F. McCoy

Soul Mate

My soul, never rests.....

Why is that?..... Does it feel troubled? Does it need a special touch to hold it at night, like a delicate blanket, to soothe over the pain and worries?.....

My soul never rests

    as you can guess

It will seek high and low

    until it begins to glow

What does it need to be bright again?..... Does it need to be seen by a special person, to make it feel beautiful and elegant like a young princess?.....

My soul never rests

    because of this sacrifice

It must pass a test

    to have its lovely price

What price is it searching for?..... To what extreme will my soul continue to seek for that prize?.....

My soul never rests

    even if it's late

For this I must contest

    it really needs its mate

Vanessa F. McCoy

LISTENING TO THE BEATS

Listen to the beats of the song, the high and low notes...Do you notice how they work together?...One note follows behind the other one, and once they are joined together the music sounds better...

Now listen to the beats of your heart...the thump, thump after thump, thump...Do you notice how they work together?...A message can be formed if you put the beats together. Just close your eyes and listen with your ears...as the beats guide you to your soul mate...

HOW DO YOU...

How do you let go of someone you never had especially when you started developing feelings you never planned to?

How do you let go of someone you may have held a few times that made you feel warm and safe on the inside?

How do you let go of someone you may have smelled a few times that made you float on air even though your feet stayed on the ground?

How do you let go of someone you may have touched a few times that made you want to lay on them forever and let time pass you by?

How do you let go of someone you may have tasted a few times that made you think you were going to melt in his mouth?

How do you let go of someone that was inside of you a few times that made you feel whole and complete like nothing in this world could ever do?

How do you let go of someone you never had that made these feelings exists like no other man could ever have?

How do you let go of someone you never had especially when you want a relationship beyond "Just Friends"...

YOU REMIND ME...

You remind me of someone I once knew
   that made all of my dreams come true
He did things for me
   that only I could feel and see

My body was caressed with care
   as each moment became a dare
My heart was opened to beauty
   with fun and laughter so truly
My eyes were filled with joy
   that became a habit to enjoy
My mind was something to explore
   with adventures that he could adore

As I gaze into your eyes
   I see something I can recognize
It's more than just a dream to me
   because it's my private and personal reality

Vanessa F. McCoy

Am I Suppose To?

Who do you think you are
 pulling some bullshit like that
As you pulled up in your car
 and got out at the drop of a hat

Am I suppose to forgive your ass
 like everything is fine and dandy
Letting you fulfill your stanky task
 with or without some damn candy

Am I suppose to jump up and down for joy
 cause you had to come and see
And say, "I'm so happy, ahoy!"
 that you came to visit me

Metamorphosis Love: Pleasant Dreams & Wishes Vol. 2

Am I suppose to let it all go
   cause so many years passed by
And just go with this fucking flow
   forgetting my years of tears and cry

Am I suppose to ignore how I was dissed
   as you made love to that bitch
And pretend like it's you I really missed
   when I should kick you in a fucking ditch

Just stop and think for a minute
   and tell me what you would do
If you wasn't in it
   cause you really have no damn clue

Vanessa F. McCoy

Do I, Should I

Do I see you as a friend

as if nothing came to an end

Do I still have feelings for you

as if I'm trying to give some damn clue

Should I pretend like I care

as you popped up from no where

Should I keep chatting with you on the phone

or enjoy being all alone

Do I still have feelings for you

only you..wish I do!!!

Feelings

U make me laugh

   U make me shout

U make me smile

   U make me pout

U make me giggle

   U make me cry

U make me happy

   U make me reply

So many feelings

   You bring out in me

None of it's bad

   Cuz you set me free

Vanessa F. McCoy

Your Eyes

Trust, respect, honor

Love, romance, sensual

Peace, calm, patience

Precise, concise, assertive

Safe, secure, guard

No matter what you say

No matter what you do

There's **POWER**...*in your eyes*

When You

When you let go of someone you never had

   your eyes and mind open up to so much you never knew.

When you let go of someone you never had

   you allow space for growth and development.

When you let go of someone you never had

   you learn more than what you thought you knew.

When you let go of someone you never had

   you really see what's always been there.

When you let go of someone you never had

   they were always there growing and developing just like you.

When you let go of someone you never had

   the truth is, they were never gone cuz they are what you have.

Vanessa F. McCoy

A Good Day

Today was a good day

    to sit, relax, and chill

Today was a good day

    to feel the natural thrill

Today was a good day

    to feel the perfect breeze

Today was a good day

    to unwind with ease

Today was a good day

    to let go of crazy stress

Today was a good day

    girl, you are blessed!!

Remember

Remember the tears
  and the fears
Remember the pain
  nearly drove you insane
Remember the crime
  what a waste of time
Remember the chase
  or was it a race
Remember crying
  from trying and trying
Remember the embarrassment
  you deeply resent
Remember it disappeared
  like you feared

Vanessa F. McCoy

Remember you let go
   flying solo
Remember you were scared
   because you cared
Now let this dissolve
   cuz it's been solved
Release this stuff
   with one big puff

Kick it out there
   any place, any where
When it comes to you
   remember it's threw
Cuz it's the past
   that didn't last
Laugh and have fun
   whether or not you see a sun

Let the world see

   you're so happy

Continue to feel

   o this love is real

Enjoy each day

   laughter is the way

Vanessa F. McCoy

Notes

Microsoft Word. Vers. 2006. N.p.: Microsoft Corporation, 2006. Computer software.

OTHER BOOKS BY VANESSA F. MCCOY

Metamorphosis Love:

The Beginning

Vol. 1

Metamorphosis Love:

Tangible Love

Vol. 3

About The Author

While many people like to get straight to the point, she's all about taking the scenic route—in writing and in life. What started out as a favorite pastime and hobby has turned into a passion for Vanessa F. McCoy, author and motivational speaker. Through her love for poetry and prose, McCoy is committed to winning lost souls for Christ, helping men and women worldwide to transition from the kingdom of darkness into the light. From short stories and novels, to plays and poetic compilations, McCoy strives to be a mouthpiece for God's kingdom—encouraging the married and single alike to live a life of integrity according to God's Word.

As a single young mother of two, she knows firsthand what life is like when you've looked for love in all the wrong places—and yet end up emotionally and spiritually bankrupt. Releasing her debut eBooks, *Metamorphosis Love: The Beginning Vol. 1* and *Metamorphosis Love: Pleasant Dreams & Wishes Vol. 2*, in 2015, and *Metamorphosis Love: Tangible Love Vol.3*, in 2017, McCoy deals with the lost and found of life and love—God's way. She's currently working on *Metamorphosis Love: Enduring Love Volume 4* and her sophomore project, *Lost Between the Tides*. After surviving numerous empty relationships, broken heartedness and emotional baggage, she's dedicated her life to inspiring others to know that a life lived outside of the will of God doesn't equate to truly living at all.

In addition to graduating magna cum laude from Wayne County Community College, she is a member of Phi Theta Kappa International Honor Society and Aspiring Writers Association of America. After competing in a Table Topics Speech Contest in The Toastmasters Club, where McCoy and others had to deliver impromptu speeches, she came in second place at the area level. Serving as a host in the Women's Ministry Small Group at Word of Faith International Christian Center in Southfield, Michigan, her authenticity, compassion for women, integrity and dedication speak loud and clear to all whom she comes in contact with.

In the times where she forgot what real love felt like, she went back to her first love—writing. For more information, please email wordswithinme@yahoo.com

www.ingramcontent.com/pod-product-compliance
Lightning Source LLC
Chambersburg PA
CBHW061302040426
42444CB00010B/2479